Paper Birds

by Don Brandis

For information contact:
Unsolicited Press
Portland, Oregon
www.unsolicitedpress.com
orders@unsolicitedpress.com
619-354-8005

Cover Design: Kathryn Gerhardt
Editor: S.R. Stewart

ISBN: 978-1-950730-76-6

Some of these poems have been published previously.

'Reviewing Mt. Wallace' and 'Thoreau's Work' were published in *The Hamilton Stone Review,* 'The Coal Cellar' in *Bone Parade,* 'Picking Rhubarb' in *Poetry Quarterly,* 'A Rainy Day's unFinish' in *Clementine Unbound,* 'landscapes' in *Red Fez,* and 'my other voice' in *Haiku Journal.*

Introductions

the words are never right esp. at first
but what else do we have?
we might have met at lunch shared a pitcher
there's a script but it's enormously and minutely unwritten
you listen while I read both parts
now and then you shrug, clear your throat
make disbelieving faces
wondering which part is yours
pages turn and you think you hear a word or two
of your own   driving your Dad's old pickup
home late on an icy road   skidding   crank the wheel
still skidding toward an oncoming bus
you open your mouth to scream
but it's a different you becoming page by page
their, your unwritten context shivers
as an unseen aurora offering

Contents

Paper Birds

Don't Tell Me

about your now-imaginary childhood
in primary-colored forest where you learned trees' silent
      communion
breathing in atmospheric hope breathing out redemption
having words for neither
don't tell me your coming-of-age in an urban swamp
of words, maligning and replacing the forest
with wave upon wave of concrete and steel
each one larger than the last; you walked
but no longer on the earth, light came and went
but no longer in the sky, only as words
smoke and tinsel to distract from what could never be said
swimming, floating, walking the bottom of grief's ocean

don't tell me how you blame yourself
for naivety as if it were a disease
those trees now wear rings of older season's dress for its
      current eye
which ever so slowly undresses them

Euridice

on black sand a mile down in the Black Sea
where no light reaches rest the bones
of a small ship lost in the 9th century
it rests as it fell to the seabed resettled
not intact yet no more damaged
than when it sank like a traumatic memory
whose passions have slunk away in centuries

her decks are memory of ax and adz,
of shipboard ways of water-walking
her sides and keel are memory of buoyancy
of half-sharing the sea's pitch and roll
wallowing and surging she storm-dives into one last wave
does not recover, her inner spaces filling with water
long held at arm's length like a conflicted lover
half-sharing, gaming the water
her weight now working against buoyancy
drifting into measureless silence

we are her last passengers unexpected
in a thousand living might-be's we hover on her
the clinical stare of the submersible
caught as her photo in the Times
her life and ours a moment of shared textured stillness

found sleeping naked on the couch wrapped in a long
        brown coat
she opens one green eye and studies me
'Orpheus?' she says, or maybe 'Coffee?'
a few gravelly syllables in an unknown tongue
her smile a sail filling in an easy wind

Toad Song

"The entire universe is the dharma body of the self."
—Dogen

The smaller i am the larger my song
the larger i am the smaller i become
when my waist is the equator
i know my legs will soon be shorter than a gnat's
soon with no parts i will fly undirected
out beyond forethought where the world is made
buoyant despite our native darkness
not the dreadful darkness of despair
but the darkness twinned by joy's slow thick light
at the quiet center where wrens sleep
despite a toad's life of grief and the burden each carries
debris of passages in an old canvas sack

protons traveling at the speed of light
near the ever-receding rim of the universe
separating into quarks shedding their Joycean name
spreading their colors briefly while losing them
all but mass-less, lighter than a thought
fading in and out of imagination
i am rim, journey, universe, proton, quark, toad

once i was walt whitman; now poetry is just poetry
a croak is just a croak, a hop is not a leap

Karma Plastic

it came not in the mail but in a plain brown mailer
set against the front door one morning
inside was a stark white card with my name on it
in an ordinary script, along with too-simple instructions
it would delay any repayment to a future lifetime
not just of misspent money, of any foolish squandering
hangovers, coronaries, and SDTs forwarded
into an unseen but all-too-certain future
even speeding tickets, burglaries, embezzlements
just hand the clerk your card as if you were a billionaire
when using it there were hints of a future in a very dark place
unknowable at first as when perceptions fade out
leaving an oddly familiar landscape of intuitions
thick forest and hovering sky, ocean pacing without sound

Christmas Voices

the old earth spun out and away into the cold
the everywhere soulless emptiness
outside this ordinary moment of light
when snow began falling in crisp one-note singles
we tried singing them so but they fell apart
needing weighted spin and drag
needing each other needing us and the hovering, trackless
      beyond

then within the house its spaces bent around us
we breathed its passive air alive
the tree held out its many arms for our baubles
we ate and drank, we sang; we called it Christmas
the moment of extraordinary light when we saw it
first of many sightings each joyful in their multitude
with matchless voices only deep silence allows

Waiting Rooms

fold around a reception desk like a small lake around a dock
when watched their corners round and blur
       to lake-like shimmer
rippling and flashing while pale painted leaves
caught and framed endure a long fade into memory

in a corner a tall pottery jar, copper-colored
like those holding Dead Sea scrolls asleep for centuries
slowly accumulating bat guano in lightless caves
this one sprouts three long sticks like young trees
in which a bright red paper bird perches
singing its paper song undisturbed by hearing

next to it hovers a huge copper owl
its wings fancied at a hummingbird's pace
rolls its tennis-ball eyes at the redbird's peerless song
the copper owl mocks our impatience
our restlessness, deafness

The Moon's Answer

a slow day mystery keeps its pages close
for turning backwards or pausing hours, weeks
      come back and it will be waiting
you marked a meeting place and haven't forgotten
who the dead were, who the living are, why it matters

a plot turns dull people into compelling corpses
an unexplained death makes them celebrities for a few days
a splash beginning of a long dive into forgotten

the deeper question, why death at all?
is sternly re-buried with discovery of this death's why
or is it justice done, or vengeance
restoring the deceptive calm of the ordinary

a splash that drew us quickly refolds itself
as the lake's plain surface over a depthless void
relaying the moon's answer

'Enough'

don't gobble, said the stream
a voice like a chorus of zippers in a melodrama
of muttering motors on an over-burdened two-lane
borrowing neighborly voices and not returning them
summer bees feeding in the raspberries
a waterfall swollen with winter excess
a tabernacle choir of 3 AM worries

a little is enough
more confuses

a dewdrop a blade of grass ask
what is enough?
they offer a hint:
'Enough' is the original act of emptiness

not three plates of spaghetti, replies the toad
with three glasses of merlot?
not ten residences in ten cities
a private jet, a trophy spouse,
a secret bank account in Panama?

they sigh, offer another hint:
cluelessness is near emptiness

Signifying

"A sage is without a self and yet nothing
is not himself/herself."
—Hongzhi

On clear days the mountains to the east
mock-threaten us as a row of whale teeth
paired with an equally toothy western range
like a jaw of an ancient whale the size of several counties
perhaps just the lower jaw, or both wide-open
stretched flat, long-dead but signifying
the snap-shut passage that awaits us
an alligator roaring up out of a quiet Florida swamp
toward a terrified child

a bear trap with cruel jaws poised
baited with a long-spoiled chunk of beef
eaten by clever crows who avoid the trigger
forgotten season after season while its springs decay
its purpose fading, settling into irony and then emptiness

some things cannot be forgotten, sink back into the
        memory-bog
below awareness where there are no losses
only additions to a waiting apocalypse

Sitting patiently in a canoe on a chilly morning lake
pretending to fish, pole and line held limp, when
a chink opens in the placidly-imagined Holocene
and the hot breath and cold eye of a new age
pass over and through us like a plague
a withering time of near-simultaneous burn and freeze
of voracious deserts and drowned cities

the morning comes on grey and slow
a steady indifferent rain seen desultory
except the single moment of the chink
not blocked now by Caesar's ashes
a moment first of birth-and-death stark as either
then behind or within it a widening space
brushing aside greater and smaller
for the 'just this' of galaxies and bacteria
self-lit to diamond clarity
startling the old you out of an enfolding X

the mountains are the momentary tips
        of a hawk's wings in flight
where its end-feathers flare near vertical
at the beginning of each down-stroke

Slow Learners

standing on bare earth
below where the kitchen was, looking at burned walls
flooring gone, rooms gone this side of the house's center
windows gone to unfiltered openings
I listen for what the house is saying
for it was never silent; giving it time
there are articulate as well as inarticulate silences
it's cold here as well as quiet
a cemetery silence, the ashes of the dead
laid long forgotten in an old piece of ground
the dead having moved on leaving debris of passage
to be rejected, forgotten by three generations
as hints now for non-relatives

death teaches the uses of forgetting
to slow learners like us, clinging like mollusks
to a narrow slice of a moment's melon
while each moment a small forgetting passes
        us blind into an unbaked miracle of light

tonight in the burned house a weak glow from streetlights
        and a vagrant moon
show us accumulated the bare beginnings of forgetting
here's winter forgetting into winter, spring into spring

The Coal Cellar

The house muttered secrets in seven languages
in its sleep creaking and sighing deep in the night
shifting on its bed of brick pillars
four feet above the black earth
a memory of the river's visits
now a mile away and tamed by dams

perhaps before but certainly after
we outgrew homes and left them
not knowing how much like turtles we are
carrying our original shell on our backs
unseen, its familiar weight unnoticed
even when we pull back into it in sleep

the divided darkness we find everywhere
frees us neither fast nor slow to live as brilliant self-lit space
       neither large nor small
she said sibilant, her smoky eyes half-closed

beside the whole dark earth our only formal cellar
was a narrow cell for a furnace and a coal bin
black lumps rumbled in streams from a dump truck
weekly, and at first were shoveled into the furnace
by a tall man in overalls, soon replaced

by a fat green slug of a feeder whose electric hum
the furnace's breathy song swallowed as coal swallows light
absorbing, becoming even the witnessing eye

combustible and nearly weightless like styrofoam
it crumbled easily in a hand as though it had no interior
only repeated exteriors of soft fine black sand
we found on every neglected upstairs surface

we burned the earth's dark jewelry as unacknowledged
          offerings to power,
like Inca children thrown into a volcano

Columbus Day

winds grapple the old house like a mad TV wrestler
facing a skilled passive fighter
the one screaming, pounding, blasting at wrinkled windows
loudly whining the metal seal around the front door
trees topple toward us heavy and slow
across the lawn wide enough to spare us
we huddle in the back of the house away from its attack
our hair on fire, trying to put it out with silence

the other, the house, depends on skillful silence
       to break the storm
through wind-loud hours it has not replied
while the storm sets upon it like a violent mind-body on
itself through surrogates, breaching a string of symbols
Moby Dick staving in the Pequod after smashing its longboats,
Napoleon barely breaching the Russians at Borodino;
of his huge army only three in a hundred survive
       their retreat from Moscow
Joan of Arc watching the flames of her murderous passions
       burn back over her
the old house flexes, slips blasts as clusters of punches
       refusing to respond or be injured

a storm needs a house to answer
a home to frightened winds
that hears what they can't ask for

sometimes home is a virtual stance hidden in bitter argument
of persons hurting
not quite ready to learn to listen

The Failing, the Falling

> "To study the self is to forget the self."
> —Dogen

the challenge is to follow as the pixels spread
and a slow falling-through appears
seen to have been active all along

having seen in our race of house-painters
        at least a dozen major flaws
as well as several dozen minor ones
well-illustrated over decades recent and distant
helps to let go of their supposed owners
if only for a few fully-engaged moments

as when one day we (formerly I) walked beside a tame lake,
picked up a small ebony stone
the size of a kidney bean or the eye of a blackbird
drawing in daylight and our re-seeing, returning nothing

the pocketed stone may have had no buoyancy to lend
perhaps an abandoned 'I' leaves only a feather's-weight
but we can imagine, unlike the clouds
that not long afterwards began to float

like swamp gas over an unpainted world
like a shared eye without intention or imagination
an eye whose reception adds nothing

to colorless neighborhoods of endless cities
to nameless rivers and highways
to speechless fields and prairies, to badlands

until after countless sightings noted
with the faintest of impressions entirely without recognition
there arose an otherwise unmarked sea of belonging

not ownership; which had gone the way of 'I'
but very like compassion which does not need
but uses and discards all marks beyond singularity

A Rainy Day's unFinish

when its early signals are ignored like winks and blushes,
it signs into distracted minds
as a flock of sparrows pecking at the roof
here and there at first then indiscriminate
drumming that rises, falls
filling up a primordial emptiness
with splashy gestures of an unfinished moment
declaring itself unfinished in crisp detail
hundreds of blur-streaks try to erase the scene
outside our windows, failing but continuing
as if to say, you're not seeing this
O blinkered men of Haddam
for we are at least a plague of locusts
come to ground as seven-foot snakes churning
wearing dozens of leathery batwings twirling for show
in a carnival you've never heard of
with crackling lightning booming thunder
while we hack like claws of blackbirds
at your roof and windows
we are your chthonic cousins
behind, beneath, within your costumes
here to the unfinish: first seeing to last unseeing
the depth of a clear night sky

A Fiddle Tune

a Mother's day is over when it starts like a song
that closes the show   her kids are grown and gone

moved to Santa Fe and Phoenix   seldom write
but no one does now   Internet illiterates

she's on the road, a fiddle in a bluegrass band
last week a gig in Nashville this week Memphis

they don't need mothering, she says
loved them but never liked them much

she plays The Ashokan Farewell and we cowboy clap
don't do it for yourself and it won't cost you much

the you that counts costs is hardly there
it's easy as falling off a roof twice

second time on crutches   she grins
we laugh remembering her feral children

Board Work

he shoulders the heavy longboards into his workshop
sets to planing them smooth
hoping they would speak to him
they will not
he usually has some sense of what is coming
before he makes a cut
so he waits
while the boards mess with him
sending out contrary fragrances of oak and pine
of hemlock, fir, birch, cedar
changing grain and color
one day they would melt like ice on the Platte in late spring
        leaving sticky puddles on the floor
another day burst into red-and-orange flames
        each with a pale blue center
into smoke and blisters bleeding heat
blackening, curling, then shrinking into cold grey piles of ash
another day morphed into a grand piano
lacquered shiny black pounding out Beethoven
delicately floating Mozart above the sawdust floor
while his tools danced and sang in German

he knows day after day the boards
only lie flat as death on his workbench

doing nothing, showing how nothing is done
still hint-blind and despairing, he thinks:
maybe I'll try Zen or poetry
the longboards, having become flooring
      sit up pointing at him, snickering

A Recurrent Aside

a notched corner at an intersection
where two buildings end, one a little shorter
leaving a space a few evergreens have filled in
over a high curb the earth mounds up to where trees cling
      as the streets drop away

what keeps returning wants something
or has something to give away
the notch faces east, gets only early morning sun
is in shadow most of the day
a deep pocket back by a molar

the evergreens are lush and silent
in a space made useless by the buildings' mismatch
too small for a parking lot, not big enough
      for a third building
a cafe, a latte stand maybe, with no crowd for either
only a few hundred yards from the prairie

the thorazine silence of invisibly wounded vets in the wards
replaces their screaming and howling
but does not heal; no one knows what would heal
      their manufactured suffering
unless there's a hint in this neglected crotch

where brick walls misalign fir and pine thrive
on a splash of morning sun savored all day
       in uncaused stillness

Chicxulub

suddenly familiar dashboard knobs on an old car
rub their ribbed surfaces against my fingers
from a distance, their upper surface's shiny vortex
set to reminding me but paused
memory's reactionary flow stunned by the Now

rows and rows of shiny fifty-year-old cars
aligned proudly in an old church parking lot
usually nearly empty even on Sundays
waxed, babied, crooned over, repainted
re-chromed, rebuilt street-legal
pretending agelessness with a nostalgia fix

from their tailpipes hop dozens of tiny dinosaurs
no bigger than tree frogs at first, though quickly
        they are larger than the cars
larger than houses, stomping gleefully on the cars
        whose owners have vanished
their cars paint-pots bright with fresh-mixed colors
lifted two at a time by one of the dinosaurs
twice the size of the old church with a delicate face
        and small agile hands
a tattoo on one leg reads 'Chicxulub"
she gives us a knowing look then sets the pots

beside the old church
takes a small tree she's plucked from the ground for a brush
she begins to re-paint the roof
in steps that aren't sequential
are all-at-a-very-thick-once

a many-coated white-wash of forgetfulness
an innocent high blue sky stripped of fifty years of discontent
a stand of grey mountain wisdom
remote, serene, waiting in shadow to be discovered
a theatrical sea with waves moving like props
    lifted and lowered by stagehands
a sullen landscape of a pre-teenager at the lip
       of the lowest ridge of mountain wisdom
       a half-step up from horizontal
and having none of it; holding her breath until she faints

Picking Rhubarb

A ring of green hands reaches for sunlight
from a pale center between root and stalk
the big leaves poisonous, the stalks tart and delicious
a deep crimson burning like an erotic blush
stalks gripped low near the ground and twisted
pulling, tear way with a crisp low sound
like a dozen pages torn in half together
showing a white scoop-like base
part of a center dissolving
like a roof pulled apart in a storm
just a moment of flow, all intensities and adverbs
gleefully, glibly, ponderously, stubbornly
like a team of synchronized swimmers whose legs and feet
then arms and hands form flower patterns
briefly before a closing splash
it is flow we see and yet do not;
we see what we've made of the broadleaf plant
not unnamed moving root-to-leaf through an unwatchable
          center
whose light routinely blinds us
unseen is the flow of us as its twinning
neither of us more than a breath
fogging winter's cold window

Mornings

sunlight re-painting the leaves
on the far side of the big maple out front
from their drab rain-country green of old fatigues
into loud excited faces at a ball game or a concert
faces shining back in uneven, fragmenting rows
or would on days of full sun
on half-lit days like this the leaves
are faces at a public lecture only a few are following
others bored, distracted, falling into themselves
        as aimless mind-wandering

it could be morning if and when we wish one,
        if it wished us back
a few are costly openings
others are sun-stained leaves dragging us along with their
        attention
as one looks up, soon all are looking up at nothing much
beginnings are so commonplace, we think
        everybody's got one
as if they were the births of strangers
we walk away from slapping imaginary dust from our hands

can we begin without knowing it?
how else would we still be here, a zillion beginnings later?

microbes in our gut, neurons flashing
incremental growth of hair and nails
long strands of memory modified by each visit
most beginnings are ingredient strangers
        sliding in beneath our distracted notice
a dog's low gargle, the moon's sly eclipse
last Friday's barbecue sizzle trio
        with aspen-leaf-and-broad-stream rustle
other beginnings wake the whole of us
any morning that wants us to can be
as Rilke's panther, Basho's frog, Buddha's flower

Brueghel Space

a Brueghel space framed by comfort-colored buildings
a medieval village square paused between filling and emptying
        by two rival groups of marchers
the first a party crowd oozing out of an inn
where a mural of a masterwork has been faithfully copied
        onto a blank wall
joining a boisterous parade, watching a bawdy sideshow,
marching with swollen bellies wearing cooking pots
wearing necklaces of bread rolls
wearing whites and reds, silly hats and masks
led by a fat man riding a barrel
balancing a meat pie on his head
holding a roast pig on a spit like a lance

the other crowd is somber, trudging out of a church
long lines of brown-hooded figures
with deformed beggars all but clawing at them
led by a thin old nun on a cart pulled by mendicants
in place of a lance she holds an oar
        with two cooked fishes on the blade

the jousters seem not to see one another
the two crowds sharing a space but nothing else

in the center of the square in a pool of sunlight
a newly-married couple walks away
out of the scene's lengthening moment
their backs to us, led by a costumed fool
they are the eyes of the crowd, the looking away
of filling from emptying, of sinking from rising

the tarted-up scene drops away into our seeing
the air around us thickens until it seems like water
then mud, then damp under-earth slowly drying out
as intense heat seeps down from above
where our world has become an incinerator
wine spilled onto the sandy floor disappears into it like time

————————————

(see Pieter Breughel's "The Fight between Carnival and Lent")

Email Karma

We at Unibody Inc are emailing
because your karma account is nearly empty
without significant new debt
you risk a zero balance
in which case, well, you can't go there
we respectfully suggest that you go slap someone
preferably a total stranger, in a public place,
   as in full of witnesses
public karma is stronger and more lasting
than private envy or vengefulness or malice
our accounting department assures us of the unlikelihood
   of a zero balance
unless you've been a saint through 40 lifetimes
have you been neglecting your body?
everything it wants needs you to exist
or it (you) become like Schrodinger's cat
since you haven't been listening to your body
try to imagine you've become both existent and non-existent
   as well as neither
as you will unless you owe someone.
You are what you owe yourself
and what you owe yourself you owe us;
the fundament of karma

Water Song

cold rain dribbles into a teacup
off the hood of my raincoat
wrinkling vision otherwise imagined clear
nearby a cup-full camp stove hisses
all night rain sang
with tent roof and sides
with trees overhead and bushes, grasses beside
with a few patches of barren hard-packed ground

percussive rain-song the only sound;
voice of all voices mocking meaning
audible to the patiently speechless
as seamless, edgeless, endless water-sound
churning rocky restless streams
boozy chuckling trickles
sea water curling in applause with briefly other-water
cut in two-hand waves by the bow of ships

sound needs another to sing
and the mating of sound in hearing:
in listening long beyond doubt and belief into knowing,
into unknowing of fruitful formlessness as all-sound

Thoreau's Work

I don't do quiet desperation
he said when he moved into a cabin
that had built itself for him
on a wooded pond a comfortable walk from Concord
he'd helped a little

at night he pulled in the pond and the trees
the sky with its many eyelets, the warm hills
and wrapped them around him like blankets
sensing otherwise they'd walk away overnight
and leave him with the Nothing

in the morning he spread them out again
in their accustomed places
sometimes he'd amuse himself and misplace them
the woods above and the sky below
laughing, they'd right themselves

he'd go for long walks in the woods
when he returned he'd sometimes find
his journal on its own had filled page after page
              with poetic silliness
which he would patiently edit until it was semi-intelligible
as close to truth as it allowed him

when he died the trees resumed their night walks
the sky and the pond would trade places, and sometimes
in the morning, in his memory, they'd stay that way
            unless somebody noticed

Ancestors

"That which sprouts buds is a dragon singing in a withered
tree."
—Dogen

A neglected small-town cemetery
surrounded by an old iron fence
has signaled No Vacancy for decades
as the town outgrew it except for their shared vacancy
no one has visited for fifty years except vandals
unless glances in its direction by passing drivers count
and repetitive speculations of idlers

Are the forgotten dead anywhere except as dust?
the flavored silence that once followed their absence
ash clinging to the tongue after a forest fire
    finally extinguished
still leaves threatened all anticipations of persistence
for the spotted owl, the Great Barrier Reef, and us

a shallow fluid 'I' walking its body from room to room
        while its other face,
strings of pulsing miracles commingled as a universe
        streaming in an abyss
of virtual gaps between there-then and here-now,

watches, lives large, remembers

vandals, passing drivers and idlers hear and don't hear
a dragon howl as rustling of spring leaves on cemetery trees

Cutting the Cat

an old yellow cat stretches
across all of yesterday
eyeing today and tomorrow
ignoring the samurai's upraised
     re-unifying blade

Free Way

set in liquid stone hardened into obedience
straight and flat as landscape allows
deep set into the earth like Roman roads
built for speed like Hitler's Autobahn
is our coming and going
through an Abyss we do not acknowledge
when It breaches as a question
we listen without knowing
we listen also in another hearing
just short of unhearing
It shows us our births and deaths
succeeding ourselves at speed
a blur of hummingbird wings
as with us, so with our concrete way
the other hearing is of 'the moon in a dewdrop'
a seeing within all seeing

Reviewing Mt. Wallace

He's lying on his back on his stone bed
paunch prominent, holding an empty whiskey glass
on his chest, snoring through pooched lips
a great poet of stony heart and solitude

he's actually three mountains
a literalist objection he'd dismiss
he's dreaming of blackbirds
in full color, in all colors
cancelling each other into perfect blackness
the emptiness of all-presence.
He smiles in the big sleep
as a thick cloud of self-vindication
erasing all those golden coaches.

Though silence is the ultimate of song
despite himself he'll sometimes stroll
among us with his loose-strung blue guitar
to sing what can be sung; the blues we are.

A poem is a moonstone, he says
(or it may have been the blackbird)
not as we are, but for itself alone

Houston Un-Mirrored

the winds didn't tell us they would stop
there is a micro-pause before beginnings
      as between heartbeats
an impending, a near-flow of yet-to
unexplored because it's hard to think between thoughts

thinking is always past, usually a small worn mirror
a rear-view glanced at sees what it gives you
if you turn your head back, then front again
you still see the dumpster you'd almost backed into
as the mirror gives but you couldn't make out,
not as your head-turned glimpse

mirror-use is also mirror-making
of resistant materials like wood planks, roof tiles, words
the unthought because unthinkable present
cannot be mirrored, can only be enacted in the eye of an act

before thinking the birds, having flown ahead of the storm
land in trees and fields a hundred miles inland
before thinking floodwaters rise up to and in through windows
      on at the ground floor of houses,
rise up in streets over the tops of cars
the waters are come for us without mirrors

The Human Circus

summer of '85 my young son and I
watch from the stands sharing a bag of popcorn
tacky with butter fat and heavily salted
coming are a line of elephants
each holding the tail of the next in its trunk
each with a human rider, a young woman
whose naked thighs grip the back of its neck
whose feet rest behind its huge ears
the size of a newspaper unfolded twice, three times
their big grey feet pad along the track just outside the rings
where the acts will be, where the fascinations
of 1850 will be invoked, and if possible, provoked
as though we had inherited them
as though the players' enchantment with them
were as infectious as Shakespeare's originals are
                  and Chaucer's aren't
the acts are all dumb-show except for the barker
bellowing every few minutes
about what we'd see if this were 1850

the animals *are* the acts, tigerish and leonine
acts with no animals are humans as trained animals
trapeze swingers in sequins agile as apes
a sword-swallower with a cruel wolf-face

a fire-eater with narrow rattler-eyes whose jaw unlocks\
      as he breaths in and spits out flames,
a troop of contortionists bending and flexing impossibly
their bizarre skills useless except to be watched
glinting off obscure fragments of the past's broken mirror

Low-Hanging Fruit

too much, too much
a modest tree overloaded with fruit
dozens of Liberty apples small and crisp
ripening slowly in the sun's long watch
crowding each other on small branches
its neighbors, other varieties having dropped their fruit
       long since
are aging parents with their children gone
watchers now, a calling little understood

each day they fall, a few at a time
ready for us some half green some in full red flush
a simple flavor tart slightly sweet
ready for us in asking
have you left off questioning for caring?
the picker leaves off pondering for eating
then for watching, then for dialogual witness

It is the Real that asks
knowing you and you it by your answer;
"I have already become like this"

Leaving with the Transcendental Self

bent Reason lashes us as itself
a tribe of passing flagellants
floundering in grief and discontent
we listen in, overhearing but not feeling addressed
not as a wall hears, a ditch, a stand of trees
not at first, not without some strange practice
stone hearing is a rare skill among humans
stone moments take in everything and give back a certified past
or the universe would not survive them
not even the uncertified, un-certifiable Transcendental Self
Death's immodest twin relentlessly ravishing and joyful
          who when one sees all see

a stone's narrow now is a spate of sounds in-gathered
and closed against us, leaving us as we were
in a snort, a shout, a single syllable
strings of these closed and joined externally
beads not speaking to each other
strung on the dimensionless present of the TS
'neither flesh nor fleshless,' the I that is the Now

autumn leaves codifying the lesser
forgetting the greater Now each nonetheless preserves

starry maple leavings red seam on yellow body
then yellow seam on red, then dirt-colorless
        in the earth's long night
falling not knowing they are clichés to us careless thinkers
though each to itself and each to each is leaving with the TS
for whom hearing is Being, for whom resemblance
        even near identity is not sameness
ask a snowflake or a grain of sand and listen

leaves adrift between branch and ground
their hot breath cooling, fading
no longer speaking to be heard but only to preserve
as though these hearings were no longer needed

Fire-Nature

from the couch we watch the fire grin at us
a caged monkey knows it can't be caged
seeming so is imaginary as cow-tipping stories
this contained fire reminds us its extended family (the McCoys)
burned down half of California this summer
we see what we are, are what we see
at the moment we are burning in a Franklin stove
playing logs-to-ashes, birth-to-death songs
to warm up the crowd for the next act
where there are no transitions only flashes
with the briefest of pauses
when studied
seem to lengthen but really slip time
like a silk robe before a bath
a fine hiss, a slither
an almost inaudible plop on an imaginary floor

we settle into fire-bath in a widening pause
what qualifiers we haven't already shed are washed/burned
      away
we burn without, burn within; burn is movement
so slow it seems unmoving, so slight it seems not to be
      happening
as if it had duration but does not

its 'slow' is intensely rapid, its 'slight' nearly cosmic
we are the heat before we feel it
are autumn-leaf-colored light dancing, dancing
are neither log nor smoke nor ash
falling outside deliberate stately like a windless snowfall
we haven't yet seen or aren't now seeing
don't recall or foresee as we choose to burn
alive and free between being and emptiness

Sources

"...in a half-baked kind of way, this cosmic welter of
attractions
was coming to stand for the real thing..."
—J. Ashbery, "The System"

trenches grown deep in an old tree's bark
like valleys dug into plains by rocks dragged under glaciers
a tree old when first seen as a child,
old seen in middle age and now in a mirroring age
      by recall's proxy
a moment crowded with near-objects pitching and flashing
from sources single, multiple and neither
sourcing has no firsts, no lasts
melts into new darkness on all sides
new is all there is; memory and hope are paradox
in a present broader than we ever see
pretending for us bite-sized sequential segments
hints in all the senses tease the mind
beyond its coat and shoes, its books and internet
no two sightings are the same yet these presume
the same object, the same viewer
a black-barked tree divided low into three trunk-sized limbs
a darkness flipping between personal and impersonal
reaching up out of perspective from a central lap

a small boy can climb into and dream
where dream and waking are neither two nor one
in recall the dark crevices aren't near enough for eye or fingers
to explore, yet a mocking immediacy persists
in pressing plainness from its side and ours
we would not be fooled, would see things as they are
say the two urgencies seeking each other
in a long courtship in and out of time
if recall seems random these urgencies are not
are felt sources seeking some kind of union neither yet knows
perhaps demonstrating what the codifying mind cannot know
      and demanding other means
since those early sightings an open future
      has become these repetitions
lost openness is one or maybe both of the urgent voices
clawing at 'this' and 'that' in our current narrow pool of light

The News Uncovered

"To lie is a small death."
—Anas Atakora

The news retails selections from slag-heaps of failed poetry
acres of mine tailings   abandoned landfills   newly turned but
about as new as Nathaniel Hawthorne mucking out stables at
Brook Farm in the 1840s   having been introduced to
pitchforks and their uses   finding his socialist fervor waning
after a few weeks. Performed video and audio by talking
mannequins who might as well be robots the news is too new
for refined uncovering by tragedy   epic   irony   too old for
purity of shock   outrage   horror   the small O'ed in-breath of
dismay. We've been trained by years of this in stock responses
disgust   boredom   titillation   sick fascination   a stoned
passivity enduring what we know to be fiction   eating cold
corned beef hash right out of the can   it's not as if *our* house
were burning. News-speak shields us from what it 'covers'
assures us we can safely ignore it   as we just have   here's
another news frito   with what looks like recycled guacamole
dip   a thousand small deaths   mosquito bites   faces too small
to be seen   tiny needles diluting and drawing   how thin
would the truth be?   the news would be a lithe young limbo
dancer

Springless

a bruised sky turns a swollen cheek, a puffy eye
spring is the asphalt in me
leaking oily fluids into rainwater
refusing to buckle to wheels and weathers
presenting as imagined
ignoring the sunlight it sucks in
making its tarry flesh seethe
preferring winter when things draw in their fragments
over spring when they grow apart

spring is the belly of a whale
dark when it would be light
light when it would be dark
haven when it would be prison
prison when it would be haven

a century from then a stranger
finds this asphalt poem this whale belly
on a page torn out of a used book
folded for a marker in another
unfolds the page; the poem puts its glasses on
and reads itself naked into strangeness

Dressing Up Dressing Down

the downslope instant diet favors us after fifty
if going uphill adds weight   going down hill
is slow fall weight loss   harder on knees and ankles
hurrying us when we would go slower
the bottom draws us when we would prolong this interval
which is only interval thereafter

all transitions are blind   even modest ones between paces
since we can only see where we are and a bit behind
could Dante foresee the reversal at the end of the Inferno?
did Jesus hanging see beyond the cross?
did Siddhartha settling beneath the Bodhi tree
to force enlightenment know what he would wake up to?

Lacking a heavy-weight imagination like some poets
a 90-pound infantry backpack hardly slowing them at all
in fact it seems to make them lighter
I have only this rucksack
at best half empty   still feeding me   the closer to empty
         it gets
the heavier it is   as though urging me to discard it

for the delights of compassionate observation

one need make nothing of   seeing its own sort of nothing
is more than enough of vital openness

everything is a story   also after the fact
it's not all that hard to just go with the flow
but if you're obstinate (required of poets) you can try prying
into the present   which is so open it overflows its opposites
seeming more closed than past or future

the present is the becoming of art
favored fiction winking its turns
trading hats until they no longer need them
faces wrestling with each other like identical twins
not over phantom priorities
but to share intensities that require each other anyway

out in the fields where no one watches, could watch
the trees and grasses dress up for spring
dress down for winter while the hare and the wolf
dress down for spring and up for winter
so we surmise from momentary sampling
walking or driving by
imagining then thinking trees and grasses
rabbits and wolves flowing yet enduring
between our samples as if we were as well

The Museum of the Herald Byrds

in the front hall near the high windows
is a portrait of Harry as the last Czar
in field uniform looking arrogant and clueless
the frame is bent and its lower right side
shows damage from a bayonet during the Revolution
paint oozes from the wound blue and khaki

the museum is mobile   does not advertise
sometimes is a sandstone estate on a bluff above the river
or a battered white box in a sub-suburban trailer park
an obscure office in the city up six floors no signage
a three-bedroom apartment in Yakima
overlooking a parking lot and a dumpster

the view's the thing   he says coughing
his voice gravelly like Dylan's who he resembles
insists he isn't the late senator from West Virginia
though if he's the late czar he could be anybody
we watch each other in an odd blue-tinged silence
a rat runs between us   when I look up again he's a woman

that's Angie   she doesn't bite   she says in a low voice
husky and cynical   almost Madonna

her fingers creeping up my leg
I get up to look at the pictures
the rooms have bare walls when you enter
then sprout dozens of small frames or a few large ones

the frames are empty until you look at them
adjusting shape size color to what appears
the baby pictures are universals
blank looks heads like misshapen pumpkins
grown with one side wedged against a fence
tiny fingers undiscovered

our hosts have vanished
seeing them at all is anomalous
since a note beside one of the frames
says they died a decade ago   their body
was never recovered   a fishing boat
sunk in Lake Superior in a storm

there are gasps from other patrons
and a few expletives   the Byrds turn up
in some photos   sitting in a bistro in Paris
sharing a table but ignoring each other
him at a loud frat party line-dancing
the Byrds weren't celebrities

who are conspicuous for going where only celebrities go
the Byrds took us everywhere

though we didn't know except now
first we'd glimpse our faces at the edge of crowds
in a photo or a painting   then two of ourselves
at different ages in the same scene

aware of each other   strangely companionable
sensing that in only a few steps we haven't noticed yet
we would begin seeing ourselves in blades of grass
in a wide field divided by a stream   in a few blossoms
rising in a patch of weeds in a neglected garden
in a flock of birds feeding on the ground in a fenced yard

in the last room is a table with a bowl of fruit
painted convex surfaces   apples pears apricots
all but bursting out of their skins
their fragrance clawing at us with desperate fingers
a fierce pockmarked sun portrait takes up
          the whole of one wall
a sly moon woman half asleep grins from another

"Contact!" – Thoreau on Katahdin

rushing toward the summit alone
walking sometimes on the tops of close-grown trees
through clouds and wind-driven rain
expecting a revelation he came instead
into a sounding wordless space of bare rock
he heard and saw with his own emptiness
the winds roar against each other
having nothing to shriek against
no trees, waves, nor corners
at first he thought he'd heard nothing
the old mountain had shed him
as it shrugged off human names
like this Anglicized Indian word for 'high place'
his own "cloud factory" would serve as well as not
he had no precedent for hearing
what it might say or not-say to him, in him
memory is mere shavings of the all-Now
he left discouraged, returning through a meadow
clustered with teeming vegetation
as had long taught him hearing, seeing
weeks later writing it up he heard with permanent hearing
what he had always sought in the woods
at Walden trains ran past him 8 times daily

in the Maine Woods' so-called wilderness
he found human hands everywhere
logging camps, clear-cut patches of forest
little settlements of a house or two with outbuildings
he sought the elusive Real no one had handled
a flow of linked oddities each stranger still
behind beneath any cultivation
in that patch of mountain meadow wind and soil
had become bushes of wild berries
forage for moose and bear and a very few human travelers
if this were cultivation then what were his scribblings
his body and mind wild and forbidding
as bare rock on Katahdin summit
what shaped them all beneath their efforts
within those too   he asked
answered   his pen-hand quivering

Originals

uncluttered attention forms a horizon
an oddity between motion and stillness
around red plastic lawn chairs waiting for spring
in a silence hinting at sound below our hearing

winter has stripped maples and birches
of their daylight leaf-songs
allowing us to hear their other singing
at first a gentler more enduring humming like classical
playing beneath spring and summer pops

we walk until we run out of descriptions
until we are just walking with no Why
among the wintering trees' barrenness
we are their older singing replayed as hearing
as we are these ordinary lines prosaic
as a parking ticket after a blind date
also replaying without names   a satisfying uniqueness
the Who of us has not sought
just walked in on   an overflow completed and shed
the next (always a next) is much like it
if originals can be said to be alike
singing of birds chasing spring from continent to continent
of sun rising and setting over delayed drowned cities

About the Author

Don Brandis is a retired healthcare worker living a happily-married hermit's life in a small town not far enough from Seattle, reading and writing poems, tending our fruit trees and meditating. He writes because good poems are invitations to engage intrinsic values in a culture that only values tools. He has published some poems with *Melancholy Hyperbole, Wild Goose Poetry Review, Red Fez, Clementine Unbound, Poetry Quarterly, The Hamilton Stone Review* and elsewhere.

CPSIA information can be obtained
at www.ICGtesting.com
Printed in the USA
LVHW021955220321
682109LV00012B/511

9 781950 730766